LETTERS FROM A CAT

PUBLISHED BY HER MISTRESS

FOR THE BENEFIT OF ALL CATS

AND

THE AMUSEMENT OF LITTLE CHILDREN

By Helen Hunt Jackson
Author of *Nelly's Silver Mine.*

with

Seventeen Illustrations
By Addie Ledyard

Design & Layout by Nancy Levey-Bossert

Written by Helen Hunt Jackson (1830-1885)
Illustrations by Addie Ledyard

Edited by Roberts Brothers (1879)

Copy Edited by Diane Hodges

Set in Watson, Williams Caslon Text provided by Adobe TypeKit
New Press Eroded by Galdino Otten

Printed in Korea

First Edition 1879
Re-print December 2019

ISBN: 978-1-7326020-5-2

E-Book ISBN: 978-1-7326020-6-9

Library of Congress Control Number: 2019946446

THE OLD MILL PRESS

Visit www.theoldmillpress.com

[Aff-*affectionate, a friend forever*]

INTRODUCTION

Dear Children:

I do *not* feel wholly sure that my Pussy wrote these letters herself. They always came inside the letters written to me by my mamma, or other friends, and I never caught Pussy writing at any time when I was at home; but the printing was pretty bad, and they were signed by Pussy's name; and my mamma always looked very mysterious when I asked about them, as if there were some very great secret about it all; so that until I grew to be a big girl, I never doubted but that Pussy printed them all alone by herself, after dark.

They were written when I was a very little girl and was away from home with my father on a journey. We made this journey in our own carriage, and it was one of the pleasantest things that ever happened to me. My clothes and my father's were packed in a little leather valise that was hung by straps underneath the carriage, and went swinging, swinging, back and forth, as the wheels went around. My father and I used to walk up all the steep hills, because old Charley, our horse, was not very strong; and I kept my eyes on that valise all the while I was walking behind the carriage; it seemed to me the most unsafe way to carry a valise, and I wished very much that my best dress had been put in a bundle that I could carry in my lap. This was the only drawback on the pleasure of my journey, my fear that the valise would fall off when we did not know it, and be left in the road, and then I should not have anything nice to wear when I reached my aunt's house. But the valise went through all safe, and I had the satisfaction of wearing my best dress every afternoon while I stayed; and I was foolish enough to think a great deal of this.

On the fourth day after our arrival came a letter from my mamma, giving me a great many directions how to behave, and enclosing this first letter from Pussy. I carried both letters in my apron pocket all the time. They were the first letters I ever had received, and I was very proud of them. I showed them to everybody, and everybody laughed hard at Pussy's, and asked me if I believed that Pussy printed it herself. I thought perhaps my mamma held her paw, with the pen in it, as she had sometimes held my hand for me, and guided my pen to write a few words. I asked Papa to please to ask Mamma, in his letter, if that were the way Pussy did it; but when his next letter from Mamma came, he read me this sentence out of it: "Tell Helen I did not hold Pussy's paw to write that letter." So then I felt sure Pussy did it herself; and as I told you, I had grown up to be quite a big girl before I began to doubt it. You see, I thought my Pussy such a wonderful Pussy that nothing was too remarkable for her to do. I knew very well that cats generally did not know how to read or write; but I thought there had never been such a cat in the world as this Pussy of mine. It is a great many years since she died, but I can see her before me today as plainly as if it were only yesterday that I had really seen her alive.

She was a little kitten when I first had her, but she grew fast and was very soon bigger than I wanted her to be. I wanted her to stay little. Her fur was a beautiful dark gray color, and there were black stripes on her sides, like the stripes on a tiger. Her eyes were very big, and her ears unusually long and pointed. This made her look like a fox, and she was so bright and mischievous that some people thought she must be part fox. She used to do one thing that I never heard of any other cat's doing: she used to play hide-and-seek. Did you ever hear of a cat playing hide-and-seek? And the most wonderful part of it was, that she took it up of her own accord. As soon as she heard me shut the gate in the yard at noon, when school was done, she would run up the stairs as hard as she could go, and take her place at the top, where she could just peep through the banisters. When I opened the door, she would give a funny little mew, something like the mew cats make when they call their kittens. Then as soon as I stepped on the first stair to come up to her, she would race away at the top of her speed and hide under a bed; and when I reached the room, there would be no Pussy to be seen. If I called her, she would come out from under the bed; but if I left the room, and went downstairs without speaking, in less than a minute she would fly back to her post at the head of the stairs and call again with the peculiar mew. As soon as I appeared, off she would run, and hide under the bed as before. Sometimes she would do this three or four times; and it was a favorite amusement of my mother's to exhibit this trick of hers to strangers. It was odd, though; she never would do it twice, when she observed that other people were watching. When I called her, and she came out from under the bed, if there were strangers looking on, she would walk straight to me in the demurest manner, as if it were a pure accident that she happened to be under that bed; and no matter what I did or said, her frolic was over for that day.

She used to follow me, just like a little dog, wherever I went. She followed me to school every day, and we had great difficulty on Sundays to keep her from following us to church. Once she followed me, when it made a good many people laugh in spite of themselves, on an occasion when it was very improper for them to laugh, and they were all feeling very sad. It was at the funeral of one of the professors in the college.

The professors' families all sat together, and when the time came for them to walk out of the house and get into the carriages to go to the graveyard, they were called, one after the other, by name. When it came to our turn, my father and mother went first, arm in arm; then my sister and I; and then, who should rise, very gravely, but my Pussy, who had slipped into the room after me, and had not been noticed in the crowd. With a slow and deliberate gait, she walked along, directly behind my sister and me, as if she were the remaining member of the family, as indeed she was. People began to smile, and as we passed through the front door, and went down the steps, some of the men and boys standing there laughed out loud. I do not wonder, for it must have been a very comical sight. In a second more, somebody sprang forward and snatched Pussy up. Such a scream as she gave and scratched his face with her claws, so that he was glad to put her down. As soon as I heard her voice, I turned around, and called her in a low tone. She ran quickly to me, and I picked her up and carried her in my arms the rest of the way. But I saw even my own papa and mamma laughing a little, for just a minute. That was the only funeral Pussy ever attended.

Pussy lived several years after the events that are related in these letters.

It was a long time before her fur grew out again after that terrible fall into the soft-soap barrel. However, it did grow out at last and looked as well as ever. Nobody would have known that anything had been the matter with her, except that her eyes were always weak. The edges of them never got quite well; and poor Pussy used to sit and wash them by the hour; sometimes mewing and looking up in my face, with each stroke of her paw on her eyes, as much as to say, "Don't you see how sore my eyes are? Why don't you do something for me?"

She was never good for anything as a mouser after that accident, nor for very much to play with. I recollect hearing my mother say one day to somebody, "Pussy was spoiled by her experience in the cradle. She would like to be rocked the rest of her days, I do believe, and it is too funny to see her turn up her nose at tough beef. It was a pity she ever got a taste of tenderloin!"

At last, what with good feeding and very little exercise, she grew so fat that she was clumsy, and so lazy that she did not want to do anything but lie curled up on a soft cushion.

She had outgrown my little chair, which had a green moreen cushion in it, on which she had slept for many a year, and of which I myself had very little use, she was in it so much of the time. But now that this was too tight for her, she took possession of the most comfortable places she could find, all over the house. Now it was a sofa, now it was an armchair, now it was the foot of somebody's bed. But wherever it happened to be, it was sure to be the precise place where she was in the way, and the poor thing was tipped headlong out of chairs, shoved hastily off sofas, and driven off beds so continually, that at last she came to understand that when she saw any person approaching the chair, sofa, or bed on which she happened to be lying, the part of wisdom for her was to move away. And it was very droll to see the injured and reproachful expression with which she would slowly get up, stretch all her legs, and walk away, looking for her next sleeping place. Everybody in the house, except me, hated the sight of her; and I had many a pitched battle with the servants in her behalf. Even my mother, who was the kindest human being I ever knew, got out of patience at last, and said to me one day:

"Helen, your Pussy has grown so old and so fat, she is no comfort to herself, and a great torment to everybody else. I think it would be a mercy to kill her."

"Kill my Pussy!" I exclaimed, and burst out crying, so loud and so hard that I think my mother was frightened, for she said quickly:

"Never mind, dear. It shall not be done, unless it is necessary. You would not want Pussy to live if she were very uncomfortable all the time."

"She isn't uncomfortable," I cried, "she is only sleepy. If people would let her alone, she would sleep all day. It would be awful to kill her. You might as well kill me!"

After that, I kept a very close eye on Pussy, and I carried her up to bed with me every night for a long time.

But Pussy's days were numbered. One morning, before I was up, my mamma came into my room, and sat down on the edge of my bed.

"Helen," she said, "I have something to tell you that will make you feel very badly, but I hope you will be a good little girl, and not make Mamma unhappy about it. You know your papa and mamma always do what they think is the very best thing."

"What is it, Mamma?" I asked, feeling very much frightened, but never thinking of

Pussy.

"You will never see your Pussy anymore," she replied. "She is dead."

"Oh, where is she?" I cried. "What killed her? Won't she come to life again?"

"No," said my mother. "She is drowned."

Then I knew what had happened.

"Who did it?" was all I said.

"Cousin Josiah," she replied. "And he took great care that Pussy did not suffer at all. She sank to the bottom instantly."

"Where did he drown her?" I asked.

"Down by the mill, in Mill Valley, where the water is very deep," answered my mother. "We told him to take her there." At these words I cried bitterly.

'That's the very place I used to go with her to play," I exclaimed. "I'll never go near that bridge as long as I live, and I'll never speak a word to Cousin Josiah, either – never!"

My mother tried to comfort me, but it was of no use; my heart was nearly broken.

When I went to breakfast, there sat my cousin Josiah, looking as unconcerned as possible, reading a newspaper. He was a student in the college and boarded at our house. At the sight of him all my indignation and grief broke forth afresh. I began to cry again; and running up to him, I doubled-up my fist and shook it in his face.

"I said I'd never speak to you as long as I lived," I cried, "but I will. You're just a murderer, a real murderer; that's what you are! and when you go to be a missionary, I hope the cannibals will eat you! I hope they'll eat you alive raw, you mean old murderer!"

"Helen Maria!" said my father's voice behind me, sternly. "Helen Maria! Leave the room this moment!"

I went away sullenly, muttering, "I don't care, he is a murderer; and I hope he'll be drowned, if he isn't eaten! The Bible says the same measure ye mete shall be meted to you again. He ought to be drowned."

For this sullen muttering I had to go without my breakfast; and after breakfast was over, I was made to beg Cousin Josiah's pardon; but I did not beg it in my heart not a bit only with my lips, just repeating the words I was told to say; and from that time, I never spoke one word to him, nor looked at him, if I could help it. My kind mother offered to get another kitten for me, but I did not want one. After a while, my sister Ann had a present of a pretty little gray kitten; but I never played with it, nor took any notice of it at all. I was as true to my Pussy as she was to me; and from that day to this, I have never had another Pussy!

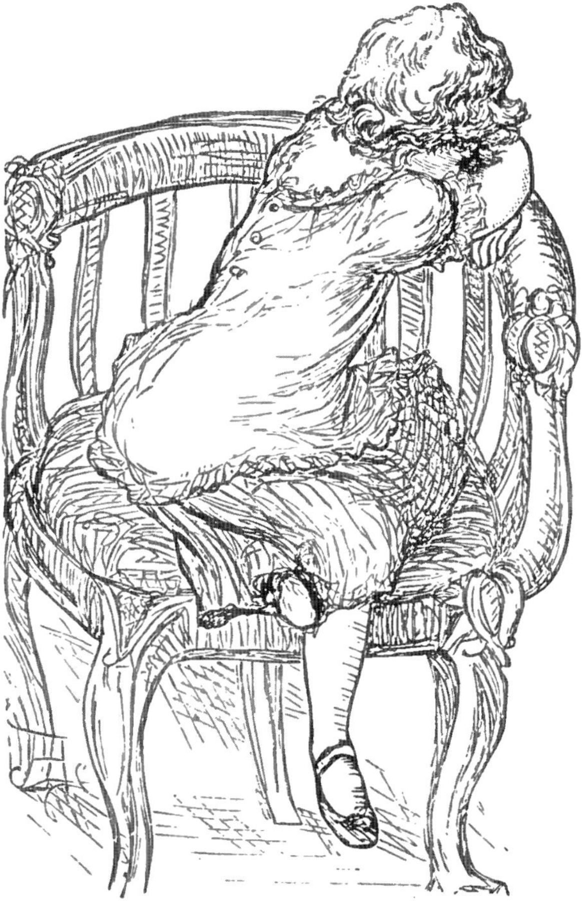

LETTERS FROM A CAT.

I.

My Dear Helen:

That is what your mother calls you, I know, for I jumped up on her writing table just now, and looked, while she was out of the room; and I am sure I have as much right to call you so as she has, for if you were my own little kitty, and looked just like me, I could not love you any more than I do. How many good naps I have had in your lap! and how many nice bits of meat you have saved for me out of your own dinner! Oh, I'll never let a rat, or a mouse, touch anything of yours so long as I live.

I felt very unhappy after you drove off yesterday and did not know what to do with myself. I went into the barn, and thought I would take a nap on the hay, for I do think going to sleep is one of the very best things for people who are unhappy; but it seemed so lonely without old Charlie stamping in his stall that I could not bear it, so I went into the garden, and lay down under the damask rosebush, and caught flies. There is a kind of fly around that bush that I like better than any other I ever ate. You ought to see that there is a very great difference between my catching flies and your doing it. I have noticed that you never eat them, and I have wondered that when you were always so kind to me you could be so cruel as to kill poor flies for nothing: I have often wished that I could speak to you about it: now that your dear mother has taught me to print, I shall be able to say a great many things to you that I have

"I felt very unhappy after you drove off yesterday."

often been unhappy about because I could not make you understand. I am entirely discouraged about learning to speak the English language, and I do not think anybody takes much trouble to learn ours. So we cats are confined entirely to the society of each other, which prevents our knowing so much as we might; and it is very lonely too, in a place where there are so few cats kept as in Amherst. If it were not for Mrs. Hitchcock's cat, and Judge Dickinson's, I should really forget how to use my tongue. When you are at home, I do not mind it, for although I cannot talk to you, I understand every word that you say to me, and we have such good plays together with the red ball. That is put away now in the bottom drawer of the little work stand in the sitting room. When your mother put it in, she turned around to me, and said, "Poor Pussy, no more good plays for you till Helen comes home!" and

I thought I should certainly cry. But I think it is very foolish to cry over what cannot be helped, so I pretended to have got something into my left eye and rubbed it with my paw. It is very seldom that I cry over anything, unless it is "spilt milk." I must confess, I have often cried when that has happened: and it always is happening to cats' milk. They put it into old broken things that tip over at the least knock, and then they set them just where they are sure to be most in the way. Many's the time Josiah has knocked over that blue saucer of mine, in the shed, and when you have thought that I had had a nice breakfast of milk, I had nothing in the world but flies, which are not good for much more than just a little sort of relish. I am so glad of a chance to tell you about this, because I know when you come home you will get a better dish for me.

I hope you found the horse chestnuts that I put in the bottom of, the carriage for

"I hope you found the horse chestnuts which I put in the carriage for you... for I had a dreadful time climbing up over the dasher with them."

you. I could not think of anything else to put in that would remind you of me: but I am afraid you will never think that it was I who put them there, and it will be too bad if you don't, for I had a dreadful time climbing up over the dasher with them, and both my jaws are quite lame from stretching them so, to carry the biggest ones I could find.

There are three beautiful dandelions out on the terrace, but I don't suppose they will keep till you come home. A man has been doing something to your garden, but though I watched him very closely all the time, I could not make out what he was about. I am afraid it is something you will not like; but if I find out more about it, I will tell you in my next letter. Good-bye.

Your affectionate Pussy.

II.

My Dear Helen:

I do wish that you and your father would turn around directly, wherever you are, when you get this letter, and come home as fast as you can. If you do not come soon there will be no home left for you to come into. I am so frightened and excited, that my paws tremble, and I have upset the ink twice, and spilled so much that there is only a little left in the bottom of the cup, and it is as thick as hasty pudding.; So you must excuse the looks of this letter, and I will tell you as quickly as I can about the dreadful state of things here. Not more than an hour after I finished my letter to you, yesterday, I heard a great noise in the parlor, and ran in to see what was the matter. There was Mary with her worst blue handkerchief tied over her head, her washing-day gown on, and a big hammer in her hand. As soon as she saw me, she said, "There's that cat! Always in my way," and threw a cricket at me, and then shut the parlor door with a great slam. So I ran out and listened under the front windows, for I felt sure she was in some bad business she did not want to have known. Such a noise I never heard: all the things were being moved; and in a few minutes, what do you think out came the whole carpet right on my head! I was nearly stifled with dust and felt as if every bone in my body must be broken, but I managed to creep out from under it, and heard Mary say, "If there isn't that torment of a cat again! I wish to goodness Helen had taken her along!" Then I felt surer than ever that some mischief was on foot; and I ran out into the garden and climbed up the old apple tree at the foot of the steps, and crawled out on a branch, from which I could look directly into the parlor windows. Oh! my dear Helen, you can fancy how I felt, to see all the chairs and tables and bookshelves in a pile in the middle of the floor, the books all packed in big baskets, and Mary taking out window after window as fast as she could. I forgot to tell you that your mother went away last night. I think she has gone to Hadley to make a visit, and it looks to me very much as if Mary meant to run away with everything that could be moved, before she comes back. After a while, that ugly Irish woman who lives in Mr. Slater's house came into the back gate. You know the one I mean, the one who threw cold water on me last spring. When I saw her coming, I felt sure that she and Mary meant to kill me while you were all away, so I jumped down out of the tree, and split my best claw in my hurry, and ran

"I climbed up the old apple tree, and crawled out on a branch from which I could look directly into the parlor windows."

off into Baker's Grove, and stayed there all the rest of the day, in dreadful misery from cold and hunger. There was some snow in the hollows, and I wet my feet, which always makes me feel wretchedly; and I could not find anything to eat except a thin dried-up old mole. They are never good in the spring. Really, nobody does know what hard lives we cats lead, even the luckiest of us! After dark, I went home; but Mary had fastened up every door, even the little one into the back shed. So I had to jump into the cellar window, which is a thing I never like to do since I got that bad sprain in my shoulder from coming down on the edge of a milk pan. I crept up to the head of the kitchen stairs, as still as a mouse, if I'm any judge, and listened there for a long time to try and make out from Mary's talk with the Irish woman what they were planning to do. But I never could understand Irish, and although I listened till I had cramps in all my legs, from being so long in one position, I was no wiser. Even the things Mary said I could not understand, and I usually understand her very easily. I passed a very uncomfortable night in the carrot bin. As soon as I heard Mary coming down the cellar stairs, this morning, I hid in the arch, and while she was skimming the milk, I slipped upstairs and ran into the sitting room. Everything there is in the same confusion; the carpet is gone; and the windows too, and I think some of the chairs have been carried away. All the china is in great baskets on the pantry floor; and your father's and mother's clothes are all taken out of the nursery closet and laid on chairs. It is very dreadful to have to stand by and see all this, and not be able to do anything. I don't think I ever fully realized before the disadvantage of being only a cat I have just been across the street, and talked it all over with the judge's cat, but she is very old and

"I crept up to the head of the kitchen stairs, as still as a mouse, if I'm any judge, and listened."

stupid, and so taken up with her six kittens (who are the ugliest I ever saw), that she does not take the least interest in her neighbors' affairs. Mrs. Hitchcock walked by the house this morning, and I ran out to her, and took her dress in my teeth and pulled it, and did all I could to make her come in, but she said, "No, no, Pussy, I'm not coming in today; your mistress is not at home." I declare I could have cried. I sat down in the middle of the path, and never stirred for half an hour.

I heard your friend Hannah Dorrance say yesterday that she was going to write to you today, so I shall run up the hill now and carry my letter to her. I think she will be astonished when she sees me, for I am very sure that no other cat in town knows how to write. Do come home as soon as possible.

Your affectionate Pussy.

P. S. Two men have just driven up to the front gate in a great cart, and they are putting all the carpets into it. Oh dear, oh dear, if I only knew what to do! And I just heard Mary say to them, "Be as quick as you can, for I want to get through with this business before the folks come back."

III.

My Dear Helen:

I am too stiff and sore from a terrible fall I have had, to write more than one line; but I must let you know that my fright was very silly, and I am very much mortified about it. The house and the things are all safe; your mother has come home; and I will write, and tell you all, just as soon as I can use my pen without great pain.

Some new people have come to live in the Nelson house. Very nice people, I think, for they keep their milk in yellow crockery pans. They have brought with them a splendid black cat whose name is Caesar, and everybody is talking about him. He has the handsomest whiskers I ever saw. I do hope I shall be well enough to see him before long, but I wouldn't have him see me now for anything.

Your affectionate Pussy.

"They have brought with them a splendid black cat whose name is Caesar, and everybody is talking about him. He has the handsomest whiskers I ever saw."

IV.

My Dear Helen:

There is one thing that cats don't like any better than men and women do, and that is to make fools of themselves. But a precious fool I made of myself when I wrote you that long letter about Mary's moving out all the furniture and taking the house down. It is very mortifying to have to tell you how it all turned out, but I know you love me enough to be sorry that I should have had such a terrible fright for nothing.

It went on from bad to worse for three more days after I wrote you. Your mother did not come home, and the awful Irishwoman was here all the time. I did not dare to go near the house, and I do assure you I nearly starved: I used to lie under the rosebushes and watch as well as I could what was going on. Now and then I caught a rat in the barn, but that sort of hearty food never has agreed with me since I came to live with you, and became accustomed to a lighter diet. By the third day, I felt too weak and sick to stir, so I lay still all day on the straw in Charlie's stall, and I really thought, between the hunger and the anxiety, that I should die. About noon I heard Mary say in the shed, "I do believe that everlasting cat has taken herself off. It's a good riddance anyhow, but I should like to know what has become of the plaguy thing!"

I trembled all over, for if she had come into the barn, I know one kick from her heavy foot would have killed me, and I was quite too weak to run away. Towards night I heard your dear mother's voice calling, "Poor Pussy, why, poor Pussy, where are you?"

I assure you, my dear Helen, people are very much mistaken who say, as I have often overheard them, that cats have no feeling. If they could only know how I felt at that moment, they would change their minds. I was almost too glad to make a sound. It seemed to me that my feet were fastened to the floor, and that I never could get to her. She took me up in her arms and carried me through the kitchen into the sitting room. Mary was frying cakes in the kitchen, and as your mother passed by the stove she said in her sweet voice, "You see I've found poor Pussy, Mary." "Humph," said Mary, "I never thought but that she'd be found fast enough when she wanted to be!" I knew that this was a lie, because I had heard what she said in the shed. I do wish I knew what makes her hate me so; I only wish she knew how I hate her. I really think I shall gnaw her stockings and shoes some night. It would not be any more than fair, and she would never suspect me, there are so many mice in her room, for I never touch one that I think belongs in her closet.

The sitting room was all in most beautiful order, a smooth white something, like the side of a basket, over the whole floor, a beautiful paper curtain, pink and white, over the fireplace, and white muslin curtains at the windows. I stood perfectly still in the middle of the room for some time. I was too surprised to stir. Oh, how I wished that I could speak, and tell your dear mother all that had happened, and how the room had looked three days before. Presently she said, "Poor Pussy, I know you are almost starved, aren't you?" and I said, "Yes" as plainly as I could mew it. Then she brought me a big soup plate full of thick cream, and some of the most delicious cold hash I ever tasted; and after I had eaten it all, she took me in her lap and said, "Poor Pussy, we miss little Helen, don't we?" and she held me in her lap till bedtime. Then she let me sleep on the foot of her bed: it was one of the happiest nights of my life. In the middle of the night I was up for a while and caught the smallest mouse I ever saw out of the nest. Such little ones are very tender.

In the morning I had my breakfast with her in the dining room, which looks just as nice as the sitting room. After breakfast Mrs. Hitchcock came in, and your mother said, "Only think, how fortunate I am; Mary did all the housecleaning while I was away. Every room is in perfect order; all the woolen clothes are put away for the summer. Poor Pussy, here, was frightened out of the house, and I suppose we should all have been if we had been at home."

Can you imagine how ashamed I felt? I ran under the table and did not come out again until after Mrs. Hitchcock had gone. But now

*"Can you imagine how ashamed I felt?
I ran under the table and did not come out again
until after Mrs. Hitchcock had gone."*

comes the saddest part of my story. Soon after this, as I was looking out of the window, I saw the fattest, most tempting robin on the ground under the cherry tree. The windows did not look as if they had any glass in them, and I took it for granted that it had all been taken out and put away upstairs, with the andirons and the carpets, for next winter. I knew that there was no time to be lost if I meant to catch that robin, so I ran with all my might and tried to jump through. Oh, my dear Helen, I do not believe you ever had such a bump. I fell back nearly into the middle of the room, and it seemed to me that I turned completely over at least six times. The blood streamed out of my nose, and I cut my right ear very badly against one of the castors of the table. I could not see nor hear anything for some minutes. When I came to myself, I found your dear mother holding me, and wiping my face with her own nice handkerchief wet in cold

"I knew that there was no time to be lost
if I meant to catch that robin,
so I ran with all my might and tried to jump through."

water. My right forepaw was badly bruised, and that troubles me very much about washing my face, and about writing. But the worst of all is the condition of my nose. Everybody laughs who sees me, and I do not blame them; it is twice as large as it used to be, and I begin to be seriously afraid it will never return to its old shape. This will be a dreadful affliction, for who does not know that the nose is the chief beauty of a cat's face? I have got very tired of hearing the story of my fall told to all the people who come in. They laugh as if they would kill themselves at it, especially when I do not manage to get under the table before they look to see how my nose is.

Except for this I should have written to you before, and would write more now, but my paw aches badly, and one of my eyes is nearly closed from the swelling of my nose, so I must say good-bye.

Your affectionate Pussy.

P.S. I told you about Caesar, did I not, in my last letter? Of course, I do not venture out of the house in my present plight, so I have not seen him except from the window.

V.

My Dear Helen:

I am sure you must have wondered why I have not written to you for the last two weeks, but when you hear what I have been through, you will only wonder that I am alive to write to you at all. I was very glad to hear your mother say, yesterday, that she had not written to you about what had happened to me, because it would make you so unhappy. But now that it is all over, and I am in a fair way to be soon as well as ever, I think you will like to hear the whole story.

In my last letter I told you about the new black cat, Caesar, who had come to live in the

"Judge Dickinson's cat, who is a good hospitable old soul,
in spite of her stupidity, invited me to tea, and asked Caesar too."

Nelson house, and how anxious I was to know him. As soon as my nose was fit to be seen, Judge Dickinson's cat, who is a good, hospitable old soul, in spite of her stupidity, invited me to tea, and asked him too. All the other cats were asked to come later in the evening, and we had a grand frolic, hunting rats in the judge's great barn. Caesar is certainly the handsomest and most gentlemanly cat I ever saw. He paid me great attention, in fact, so much that one of those miserable half-starved cats from Mill Valley grew so jealous that she flew at me and bit my ear till it bled, which broke up the party. But Caesar went home with me, so I did not care; then we sat and talked a long time under the nursery window. I was so much occupied in what he was saying, that I did not hear Mary open the window overhead, and was therefore terribly frightened when there suddenly came down on us a whole pailful of water. I was so

"When there suddenly came down on us a whole pailful of water."

startled that I lost all presence of mind; and without bidding him good night, I jumped directly into the cellar window by which we were sitting. Oh, my dear Helen, I can never give you any idea of what followed. Instead of coming down as I expected to on the cabbages, which were just under that window the last time I was in the cellar, I found myself sinking, sinking, into some horrible soft, slimy, sticky substance, which in an instant more would have closed over my head, and suffocated me; but, fortunately, as I sank, I felt something hard at one side, and making a great effort, I caught on it with my claws. It proved to be the side of a barrel, and I succeeded in getting one paw over the edge of it. There I hung, growing weaker and weaker every minute, with this frightful stuff running into my eyes and ears, and choking me with its bad smell. I mewed as loud as I could, which was not very loud, for whenever

I opened my mouth the stuff trickled into it off my whiskers. But I called to Caesar, who stood in great distress at the window, and explained to him, as well as I could, what had happened to me, and begged him to call as loudly as possible. For if somebody did not come very soon, and take me out, I should certainly die. He insisted, at first, on jumping down to help me himself, but I told him that would be the most foolish thing he could do; if he did, we should certainly both be drowned. So he began to mew at the top of his voice, and between his mewing and mine, there was noise enough for a few minutes. Then windows began to open, and I heard your grandfather swearing and throwing out a stick of wood at Caesar; fortunately, he was so near the house that it did not hit him. At last your grandfather came downstairs and opened the back door, and Caesar was so frightened that he ran away, for which I have never thought so well of him since, though we are still very good friends. When I heard him running off, and calling back to me, from a distance, that he was so sorry he could not help me, my courage began to fail, and in a moment more , I should have let go of the edge of the barrel and sunk to the bottom. But luckily, your grandfather noticed that there was something very strange about my mewing and opened the door at the head of the cellar stairs, saying, "I do believe the cat is in some trouble down here." Then I made a great effort and mewed still more piteously. How I wished I could call out and say, "Yes, indeed, I am; drowning to death, in I'm sure I don't know what, but something a great deal worse than water!" However, he understood me as it was, and came down with a lamp. As soon as he saw me, he set the lamp down on the cellar bottom, and laughed so that he could hardly move. I thought this was the most cruel thing

I ever heard of. If I had not been, as it were, at death's door, I should have laughed at him, too, for even with my eyes full of that dreadful stuff, I could see that he looked very funny in his red nightcap, and without his teeth. He called out to Mary, and your mother, who stood at the head of the stairs, "Come down, come down. Here's the cat in the soft-soap barrel!" and then he laughed again, and they both came down the stairs laughing, even your dear kind mother, who I never could have believed would laugh at anyone in such trouble. They did not seem to know what to do at first. Nobody wanted to touch me, and I began to be afraid I should drown while they stood looking, at me, for I knew much better than they could how weak I was from holding on to the edge of the barrel so long. At last your grandfather swore that oath of his, you know the one I mean, the one he always swears when he is very sorry for anybody, and

"He lifted me out by the nape of my neck, holding me as far off from him as he could."

lifted me out by the nape of my neck, holding me as far off from him as he could, for the soft soap ran off my legs and tail in streams. He carried me up into the kitchen, and put me down in the middle of the floor, and then they all stood around me, and laughed again, so loud that they waked up the cook, who came running out of her bedroom with her tin candlestick and a chair in her hand, thinking that robbers were breaking in. At last your dear mother said, "Poor Pussy, it is too bad to laugh at you, when you are in such pain." (I had been thinking so for some time.) "Mary, bring the small washtub. The only thing we can do is to wash her."

When I heard this, I almost wished they had left me to drown in the soft soap. For if there is anything of which I have a mortal dread, it is water. However, I was too weak to resist, and they plunged me in all over, into the tub full of ice-cold water, and Mary began to rub me with her great rough hands, which, I assure you, are very different from yours and your mother's. Then they all laughed again to see the white lather it made; in two minutes the whole tub was as white as the water under the mill wheel that you and I have so often been together to see. You can imagine how my eyes smarted. I burnt my paws once in getting a piece of beefsteak out of the coals where it had fallen off the gridiron, but the pain of that was nothing to this. You will hardly believe me when I tell you that they had to empty the tub and fill it again ten times before the soap was all washed out of my fur. By that time, I was so cold and exhausted, that I could not move, and they began to think I should die. But your mother rolled me up in one of your old flannel petticoats and made a nice bed for me behind the stove. By this time even Mary began to seem sorry for me, though she was very cross at first, and hurt me much more than she needed to in washing me. Now she said, "You're nothing but a poor beast of a cat, to be sure, but it's myself that would be sorry to have the little mistress come back and find ye kilt." So you see, your love for me did me service, even when you were so far away. I doubt very much whether they would have ever taken the trouble to nurse me through this sickness, except for your sake. But I must leave the rest for my next letter. I am not strong enough yet to write more than two hours at a time.

Your affectionate Pussy.

VI.

My Dear Helen:

I will begin where I left off in my last letter.

As you may imagine, I did not get any sleep that night, not even so much as a cat's nap, as people say, though how cat's naps differ from men's and women's naps, I don't know. I shivered all night, and it hurt me terribly whenever I moved. Early in the morning your grandfather came downstairs, and when he saw how I looked, he swore again, that same oath. We all know very well what it means when he swears in that way: it means that he is going to do all he can for you, and is so sorry, that he is afraid of seeming too sorry. Don't you remember when you had that big double tooth pulled out, and he gave you five dollars, how he swore then? Well, he took me up in his arms, and carried me into the dining room; it was quite cool; there was a nice wood fire, on the hearth, and Mary was setting the table for breakfast. He said to her in a very gruff voice, "Here you, Mary, you go up into the garret and bring down the cradle."

Sick as I was, I could not help laughing at the sight of her face. It was enough to make any cat laugh.

"You don't ever mean to say, sir, as you're going to put that cat into the cradle."

"You do as I tell you," said he, in that most awful tone of his, which always makes you so afraid. I felt afraid myself, though all the time he was stroking my head, and saying, "Poor Pussy, there, poor Pussy, lie still." In a few minutes Mary came down with the cradle

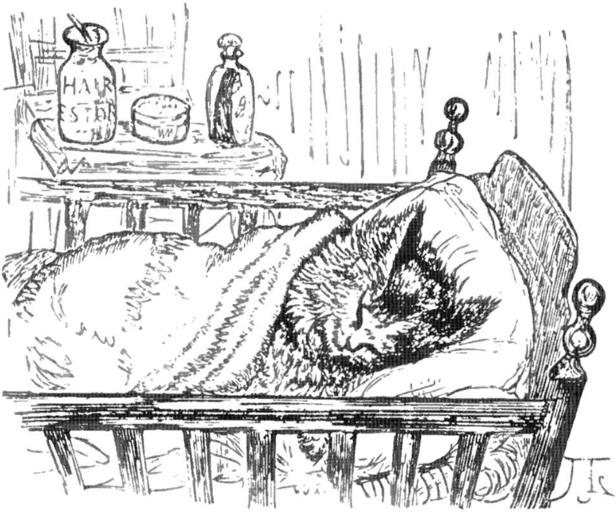

"Then your grandfather mad up a nice bed in the cradle, and me down in it."

and set it down by the fire with such a bang that I wondered it did not break. You know she always bangs things when she is cross, but I never could see what good it does. Then your grandfather made up a nice bed in the cradle, out of Charlie's winter blanket and an old pillow, and laid me down in it, all rolled up as I was in your petticoat. When your mother came into the room, she laughed almost as hard as she did when she saw me in the soft-soap barrel, and said, "Why, Father, you are rather old to play cat's cradle!" The old gentleman laughed at this, till the tears ran down his red cheeks. "Well," he said, "I tell you one thing; the game will last me till that poor cat gets well again." Then he went upstairs and brought down a bottle of something very soft and slippery, likc lard, and put it on my eyes, and it made them feel much better. After that he gave me some milk into which he had put some of his very best brandy: that was pretty hard to get down, but I understood enough of what they had said, to be sure that if I did not take something of the kind I should never get well. After breakfast I tried to walk, but my right paw was entirely useless. At first, they thought it was broken, but finally decided that it was only sprained and must be bandaged. The bandages were wet with something that smelled so badly it made me feel very sick, for the first day or two. Cats' noses are much more sensitive to smells than people's are; but I grew used to it, and it did my poor lame paw so much good that I would have borne it if it had smelled twice as badly. For three days I had to lie all the time in the cradle: if your grandfather caught me out of it, he would swear at me and put me back again. Every morning he put the soft white stuff on my eyes and changed the bandages on my leg. And, oh, my dear Helen, such good things as I had to eat! I had almost the same things for my dinner that the rest of them did. It must be a splendid thing to be a man or a woman! I do not think I shall ever again be contented to eat in the shed and have only the old pieces that nobody wants.

Two things troubled me very much while I was confined to the cradle: one was that everybody who came in to see your mother laughed as if they never could stop, at the first sight of me; and the other was that I heard poor Caesar mewing all around the house and calling me with all his might; and I knew he thought I was dead. I tried hard to make your kind mother notice his crying, for I knew she would be willing to let him come in and see me, but I could not make her understand. I suppose she thought it was only some common strolling cat who was hungry. I have always noticed that people do not observe any difference between one cat's voice and another's; now they really are just as different as human voices. Caesar has one of the finest, deepest-toned voices I ever heard. One day, after I got well enough to be in the kitchen, he slipped in, between the legs of the butcher's boy who was bringing in some meat, but before I had time to say one word to him, Mary flew at him with the broom, and drove him out. However, he saw that I was alive, and that was something. I am afraid it will be some days yet before 1 can see him again, for they do not let me go out at all, and the bandages are not taken off my leg. The cradle is carried upstairs, and I sleep on Charlie's blanket behind the stove. I heard your mother say today that she really believed the cat had the rheumatism. I do not know what that is, but I think I have got it: it hurts me all over when I walk, and I feel as if I looked like Bill Jacobs's old cat, who, they say, is older than the oldest man in town; but of course that must be a slander.

"One day he slipped in between the legs of the butcher boy, but before I had time to say a word to him, Mary flew at him with the broom."

The thing I am most concerned about is my fur. It is coming off in spots: there is a bare spot on the back of my neck, on the place by which they lifted me up out of the soap barrel, half as large as your hand; and whenever I wash myself, I get my mouth full of hairs, which is very disagreeable. I heard your grandfather say today that he believed he would try Mrs. Somebody's hair restorer on the cat, at which everybody laughed so that I ran out of the room as fast as I could go, and then they laughed still harder. I will write you again in a day or two and tell you how I am getting on. I hope you will come home soon.

Your affectionate Pussy.

VII.

My Dear Helen:

I am so glad to know that you are coming home next week that I cannot think of anything else. There is only one drawback to my pleasure, and that is, I am so ashamed to have you see me in such a plight. I told you, in my last letter, that my fur was beginning to come off. Your grandfather has tried several things of his, which are said to be good for hair, but they have not had the least effect. For my part, I don't see why they should; fur and hair are two very different things, and I thought at the outset there was no use in putting on my skin what was intended for the skin of human heads, and even on them don't seem to work any great wonders, if I can judge from your grandfather's head, which you know is as bald and pink and shiny as a baby's. However, he has been so good to me that I let him do anything he likes, and every day he rubs in some new kind of stuff, which smells a little worse than the last one. It is utterly impossible for me to get within half a mile of a rat or a mouse. I might as well fire off a gun to let them know I am coming, as to go about scented up so that they can smell me a great deal farther off than they can see me. If it were not for this dreadful state of my fur, I should be perfectly happy, for I feel much better than I ever did before in my whole life and am twice as fat as when you went away. I try to be resigned to whatever may be in store for me, but it is very hard to look forward to being a fright all the rest of one's days. I don't suppose such a thing was ever seen in the world as a cat without any fur.

This morning your grandfather sat looking at me for a long time and stroking his chin. At last he said, "Do you suppose it would do any good to shave the cat all over?" At this I could not resist the impulse to scream, and your mother said, "I do believe the creature knows whenever we speak about her." Of course I do! Why in the world shouldn't I! People never seem to observe that cats have ears. I often think how much more careful they would be if they did. I have laughed many a time to see them send children out of the room, and leave me behind, when I knew perfectly well that the children would neither notice nor understand half so much as I would. There are some houses in which I lived, before I came to live with you, about which I could tell strange stories if I chose.

Caesar pretends that he likes the looks of little spots of pink skin, here and there, in fur; but I know he only does it to save my feelings, for it isn't in human nature, I mean, in cats' nature-, that any one should. You see I spend so much more time in the society of men and women than of cats, that I find myself constantly using expressions that sound queerly in a cat's mouth. But you know me well enough to be sure that everything I say is perfectly natural. And now, my dear Helen, I hope I have prepared you to see me looking perfectly hideous. I only trust that your love for me will not be entirely killed by my unfortunate appearance. If you do seem to love me less, I shall be wretched, but I shall still be, always,

Your affectionate Pussy.